This book belongs to:

A young female horse is

called a filly

A young female horse is

called a filly.

A young male horse is

called a colt

A young male horse is

called a colt

Ponies are small horses

Ponies are small horses

A female horse is

called a mare

A female horse is

called a mare

A male horse is called a

stallion

A male horse is called a

stallion

Horses have evolved over

the past 50 million years

from smaller creatures

Horses have evolved over

the past 50 million years

from smaller creatures

Estimates suggest that there
are around 60 million
horses in the world

Estimates suggest that there
are around 60 million horses in the world

The fastest recorded sprint-

ing speed of a horse

was 55 mph

The fastest recorded sprinting

speed of a horse

was 55 mph

Horses gallop at

around 27 mph

Horses gallop at

around 27 mph

Horses are capable of seeing

nearly 360 degrees

at one time

Horses are capable of seeing

nearly 360 degrees

at one time

Horses have bigger eyes

than any other mammal

that lives on land.

Horses have bigger eyes

than any other mammal

that lives on land.

Horses are herbivores

(plant eaters)

Horses are herbivores

(plant eaters)

Horses have been
domesticated for over
5000 years

Horses have been
domesticated for over
5000 years

Horses have around 205

bones in their skeleton

Horses have around 205

bones in their skeleton

The oldest horse we know
of was named 'Old Billy'
and is said to have lived 62
years.

The oldest horse we know
of was named 'Old Billy'
and is said to have lived 62
years.

Domestic horses have a
lifespan of around 25 years

Domestic horses have a
lifespan of around 25 years

Horses can run

shortly after birth.

Horses can run

shortly after birth.

Horses can sleep both lying

down and standing up

Horses can sleep both ly-

ing down and standing up

When horses look like they are laughing, they are actually practicing "flehmen," to determine whether a smell is good or bad

Horses are better at seeing

yellows and greens than

purples and violets.

Horses are better at seeing

yellows and greens than

purples and violets.

A horse's teeth take up a
larger amount of space in
their head than their brain

A horse's teeth take up a
larger amount of space in
their head than their brain

Male horses have 40 teeth

while females have 36

Male horses have 40 teeth

while females have 36

Horse hooves are made from the same protein that comprises human hair and fingernails

Horses are more secure and

comfortable when trailering

if they can face the rear

Horses are more secure and

comfortable when trailering

if they can face the rear

From 1867 to 1920, the number of horses went up from 7.8 million to 25 million

The Przewalski's horse is the

only truly wild horse

species still in existence

The Przewalski's horse is the

only truly wild horse

species still in existence

Horses use their ears, eyes
and nostrils to express
their mood

Horses use their ears, eyes
and nostrils to express
their mood

Horses communicate their
feelings through facial
expressions.

Horses communicate their
feelings through facial
expressions.

Horses will not lie down at the same time because one will act as a look-out for potential dangers

Vocalizations are highly

important to horses.

Vocalizations are highly

important to horses.

Whinnying and
neighing sounds are elicited
when horses meet or leave
each other

Stallions (adult male

horses) perform loud roars

as mating calls

Stallions (adult male

horses) perform loud roars

as mating calls

Horses will use snorts to

alert others of potential

danger

Horses will use snorts to

alert others of potential

danger

Approximately 4.6 million Americans work in the horse industry in one way or another

An adult horse's brain

weights 22 oz, about half

that of a human

An adult horse's brain

weights 22 oz, about half

that of a human

Horses still hold a place of

honor in many cultures

Horses still hold a place of

honor in many cultures

Horses can not vomit

Horses can not vomit

There is only one species of

domestic horse

There is only one species of

domestic horse

There are around 400
different horse breeds

There are around 400

different horse breeds

Different horses breeds specialize in everything from pulling wagons to racing

All horses are grazers

All horses are grazers

A horse can see better at

night than a human

A horse can see better at

night than a human

The first cloned horse was a

Haflinger mare in

Italy in 2003

The first cloned horse was a

Haflinger mare in

Italy in 2003

Horses like sweet flavors

and will usually reject

anything sour or bitter

Horses like sweet flavors

and will usually reject

anything sour or bitter

Wild horses generally

gather in groups of 3 to 20

Wild horses generally

gather in groups of 3 to 20

Horses produce
approximately 10 gallons
of saliva a day

Horses produce
approximately 10 gallons
of saliva a day

On a horse's hoof is a
triangular shaped area
called the "frog" which acts
as a shock absorber for
a horse's leg

The tallest horse on record

was a Shire named

Sampson. He was

7 feet, 2 inches tall

The average horse's heart

weighs approximately

9 or 10 pounds

The average horse's heart

weighs approximately

9 or 10 pounds

The record for the highest

jump made by a horse is

held by a horse was 8 feet

1 and 1/4 inches

Horses with typical anat-
omy breathe through their
nostrils and cannot breathe
through their mouths.

Horses drink at least 25

gallons of water a day

(more in hotter climates)

Horses drink at least 25

gallons of water a day

(more in hotter climates)

It takes 9-12 months to

re-grow an entire

horse hoof

It takes 9-12 months to

re-grow an entire

horse hoof

Horses with pink skin can

get a sunburn

Horses with pink skin can

get a sunburn

Zebroid is a cross between a

zebra and another

member of the Equidae

Zebroid is a cross between a

zebra and another

member of the Equidae

Eduidae family includes

zebras, donkeys, ponies,

and horses

Eduidae family includes

zebras, donkeys, ponies,

and horses

A "zonky" is a cross

between a zebra and

a donkey

A "zonky" is a cross

between a zebra and

a donkey

A "zony" is a cross between

a zebra and a pony

A "zony" is a cross between

a zebra and a pony

A "zorse" is a cross between

a zebra and a horse

A "zorse" is a cross between

a zebra and a horse

You can tell if a horse is

cold by feeling behind

their ears

You can tell if a horse is

cold by feeling behind

their ears

Horses have 16 muscles in each ear, allowing them to rotate their ears 180 degrees

Horses have 16 muscles in each ear, allowing them to rotate their ears 180 degrees

If a horse has a red ribbon

on it's tail, it kicks

If a horse has a red ribbon

on it's tail, it kicks

Horses are social animals
and will get lonely if
kept alone

Horses are social animals
and will get lonely if
kept alone

Horses will mourn the

passing of a companion

Horses will mourn the

passing of a companion

What was your favorite horse fact?

What do you like most
about horses?

Do you know anything else about horses?

What is your favorite

horse color?

Who is your equestrian idol?

Describe your dream horse...

Do you have a favorite

horse breed?

Quotes about horses...

No hour of life is wasted

that is spent in the saddle.

-Winston Churchhill

A horse is worth more

than riches.

– Spanish Proverb

A horse is worth more

than riches.

– Spanish Proverb

A horse gallops with his lungs, Perseveres with his heart, And wins with his character. —Tesio

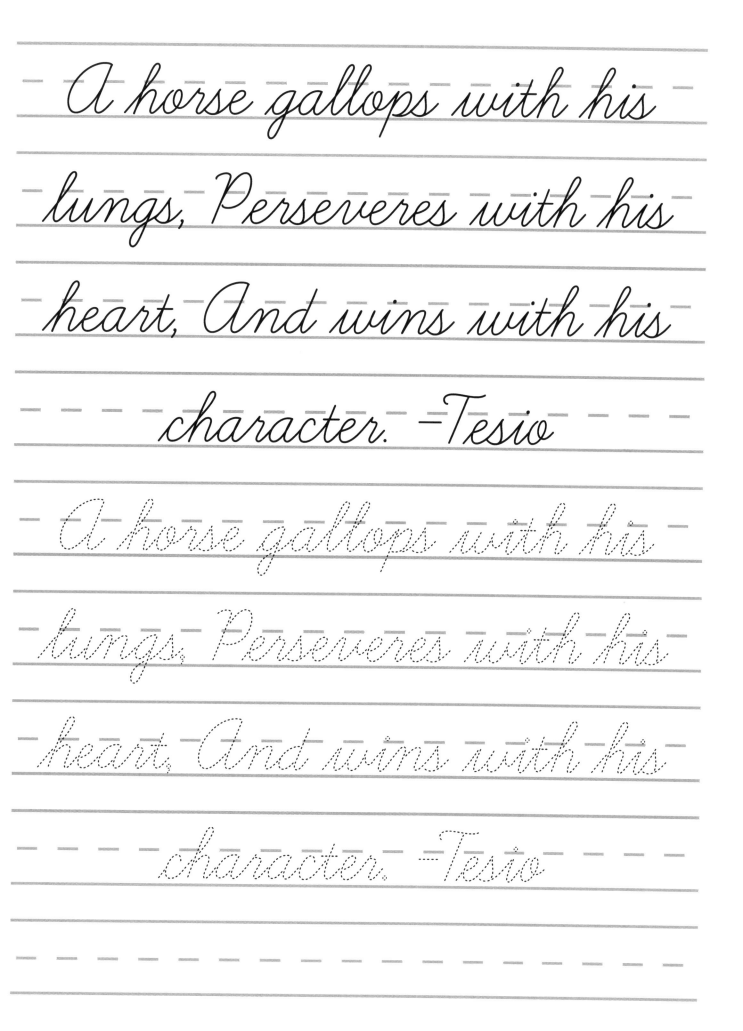

When you are on a great

horse, you have the best seat

you will ever have.

--Winston Churchill

The wind of heaven is that

which blows between a

horse's ears.

--- Arabian Proverb

Riding a horse is not a
gentle hobby, to be picked
up and laid down like a
game of Solitaire. It is a
grand passion.
— Ralph Waldo Emerson

A true horseman does not look at a horse with his eyes, he looks at his horse with his heart.

— Unknown

If the horse does not enjoy
his work, his rider will
have no joy.
— H.H. Isenbart

You cannot train a horse

with shouts and expect it to

obey a whisper.

— Dagobert D. Runes

I've often said there is nothing better for the inside of the man, than the outside of the horse.

--- Ronald Reagan

Your seat is a verb, and
your reins are adjectives to
add beauty and shape.

— Pat Parelli

I figure if a girl wants to
be a legend, she should go
ahead and be one.
— Calamity Jane

Courage is being scared to

death... and saddling up

anyway.

— John Wayne

There are only two

emotions that belong in the

saddle; one is a sense of

humor and the other is

patience.

— John Lyons

There is much we can learn

from a friend who happens

to be a horse.

— Aleksandra Layland

Horses make a landscape

look beautiful.

— Alice Walker

There is no better place to
heal a broken heart than
on the back of a horse.
— Missy Lyons

It is the difficult horses

that have the most to give

you.

— Lendon Gray

If your horse says no, you either asked the wrong question, or asked the question wrong.

--- Pat Parelli

Care, and not fine stables,

makes a good horse.

— Danish Proverb

All our dreams come true if
we have the courage to
pursue them.
— Walt Disney

And some horse jokes...

Have you heard the story about the runaway horse? It's a terrible tale of 'Whoa!'

What's black and white

and eats like a horse?

A zebra

What's black and white

and eats like a horse?

A zebra

What ailment do horses

fear most?

Hay Fever

What ailment do horses

fear most?

Hay Fever

What kind of bread does a

racehorse eat?

Thoroughbred

What kind of bread does a

racehorse eat?

Thoroughbred

Why couldn't the

pony sing?

He was a little hoarse

Why couldn't the

pony sing?

He was a little hoarse

How do you know a horse

has a negative attitude?

He always says "Neigh"

How do you know a horse

has a negative attitude?

He always says "Neigh"

Resources used to create this book:

https://www.doubledtrailers.com/45-random-amazing-bizarre-horse-facts/
https://theultimateequestrian.com/25-horse-jokes-and-puns-horse-humour/
https://theultimateequestrian.com/inspirational-horse-quotes/

Made in the USA
Middletown, DE
26 October 2023

41426674R00057